KATHRYN CAVE has written fiction and non-fiction for children of all ages in the 15 years since her first book, *Dragonrise*, was published. In 1997 she was awarded the first UNESCO Prize for Services to Tolerance in Children's Literature, for her story *Something Else* (Puffin, illustrated by Chris Riddell). She has worked in publishing for over 25 years and until recently was an Editorial Director at Frances Lincoln. She has now left to become a full-time writer. Her previous titles include *Andrew Takes the Plunge, Best Friends for Ever* and *Running Battles* (Puffin); *The Emperor's Grucklehound, Similon* and *Horatio Happened* (Hodder) and *The Boy who Became an Eagle* (DK). Her published titles for Frances Lincoln include *Out for the Count* and her previous collaboration with Oxfam, *W is for World*.

For Isis and Makeda – K.C.

One Child One Seed copyright © Frances Lincoln Limited 2002
Text copyright © Kathryn Cave 2002
Photographs copyright © Oxfam Activities Limited and Gisèle Wulfsohn 2002

First published in Great Britain in 2002 by
Frances Lincoln Limited, 4 Torriano Mews,
Torriano Avenue, London NW5 2RZ

British Library Cataloguing in Publication Data available on request

ISBN 0-7112-2075-1 paperback

Printed in Singapore
1 3 5 7 9 8 6 4 2

*Oxfam and the publishers would like to thank Nothando and her family, their community in Nkandla district,
KwaZulu Natal and Kwazi Mazibuko for their enthusiastic support.*

*Oxfam GB will receive a 5% royalty for each copy of this book sold in the UK.
Oxfam is a Registered Charity no. 202918. Oxfam GB is a member of Oxfam International.*

*Oxfam believes every human being is entitled to a life of dignity and opportunity. Working with others we
use our ingenuity, knowledge and wealth of experience to make resources and money work harder.
From practical work with individuals through to influencing world policy we aim to enable the world's
poorest people to create a future that no longer needs Oxfam.*

ONE CHILD ONE SEED

A SOUTH AFRICAN COUNTING BOOK

Kathryn Cave • *Photographs by* Gisèle Wulfsohn

FRANCES LINCOLN
In Association with Oxfam

1 One child, one seed.

Here is Nothando with her pumpkin seed. She lives in South Africa, where pumpkins grow all summer long.

Nothando lives with her Aunt Nomusa (in red) and her Grandmother Betty (in blue). Her big sister and her mother are on the right of the picture, and her brother is on the left. They live nearby and spend a lot of time with Nothando.

Two hands to plant the seed.

Nothando buries the pumpkin seed in the earth. It's November, the beginning of summer. The summer rains will help the seed to grow. By February, it will have grown into a pumpkin big enough to eat.

The homestead where Nothando lives is in a district called Nkandla. The main house has a kitchen, a living room and a bedroom.

Its walls (shown in the picture) are made of wood, mud and grass. They are then plastered and painted. The roof is corrugated iron. Outside there are three thatched huts called rondavels, used for cooking and storage.

Three ways to help it grow.

Some years the summer rains are very heavy, and the river that flows through Nkandla floods. Too much water is bad for the crops: they rot, and when the water finally drains away there's lots of clearing up to do. Women do the work by hand, with help from the children.

Nothando's brother Siphelele has a spade to dig up weeds. Their friend Nobuhle has water in her bucket to keep the little plant alive in dry weather. Nothando helps with the hoe.

Four creatures watch.

If these cows get too close they'll tread on the little pumpkin plant, or even eat it.

Who will see that they don't? Nothando's cousin Mongezi gets that job. He's the family cowherd.

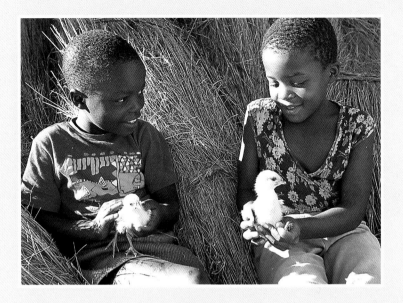

All the animals on the homestead have to earn their keep. Cows do that by giving milk and meat. Chicks provide eggs and meat once they're fully grown. Cats and dogs make themselves useful by chasing and catching rats.

5

Five friends to pick the pumpkin.

Any month can be harvest time because vegetables grow all year round. Out in the fields and in the vegetable garden you can find cabbage, spinach, beetroot, potatoes, beans and mealies (the local name for maize).

The pumpkin's stalk has dried out. That means the pumpkin's ripe. It's time for Nothando and her friends to pick it and carry it home.

Six things to buy.

Sibongile store is a ten-minute walk from the homestead. The town of Nkandla is much further, and there aren't many shops there – just a few that sell food or clothes. There's a farmers' market in the town, too.

Now it's time to turn the pumpkin into a feast! Nothando walks to the store to stock up with sugar, mealie meal, bread and margarine, and a passionfruit drink.
The curry powder is for a vegetable curry, tomorrow.

7 Seven weary walkers.

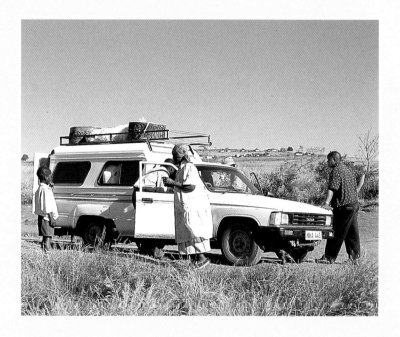

The roads around Nkandla are just dirt, and in the rainy season they can't be used. When it's not too wet, this small van runs a taxi service three times a day from outside Nothando's school into town and back again. The half-hour trip costs 6 rand each way.

The nearest big city is Durban, 300 km away. Nothando dreams of going there one day.

It's a long walk home for dinner after an afternoon in the vegetable garden. But that's the way most people get around here: on foot.

8

Eight slices of ripe pumpkin.

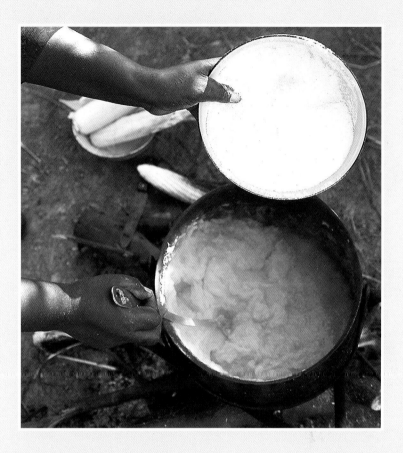

Tonight Aunt Nomusa is chief cook. First she cuts off the pumpkin's tough peel. Then she scrapes out the seeds, and cuts the pumpkin into slices. It looks a lot smaller now – let's hope there's enough to go round.

Aunt Nomusa adds mealie meal to the cooked pumpkin to thicken it, and sugar to make it sweet. The homestead has no fridge, so fresh food has to be cooked and eaten before it goes bad.

Many families can't afford to cook more than once a day, usually in the evening. Those who can, cook lunch or a midday snack too: bean soup or chicken and mealie meal. Breakfast is usually a mug of tea and some bread.

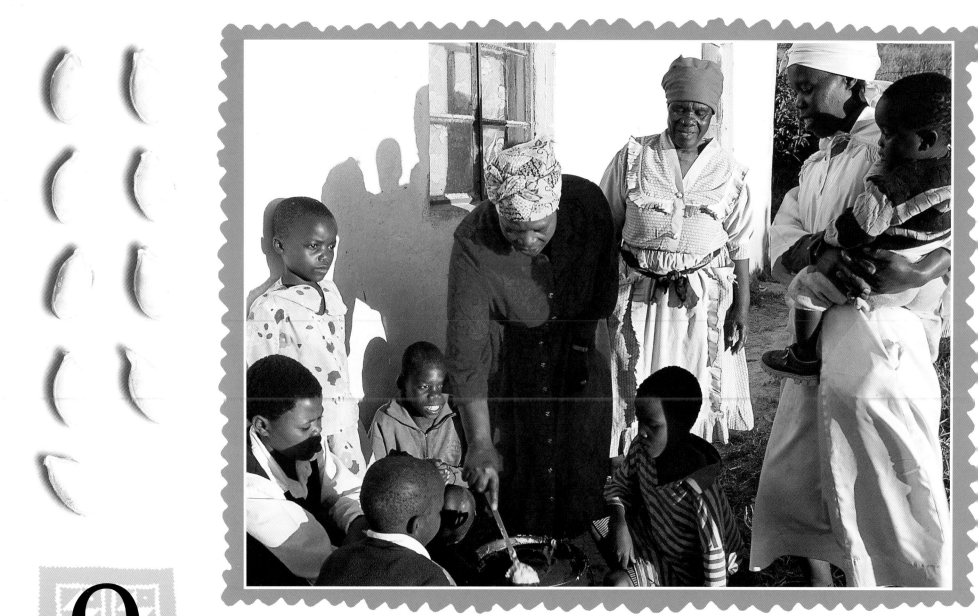

9 Nine hungry eaters waiting for a treat.

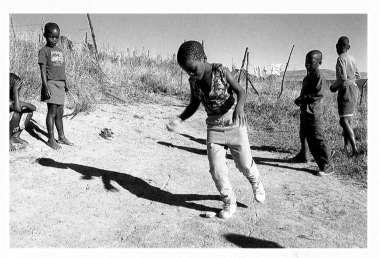

Games make the time until dinner pass more quickly. This is Am I In?, *Nothando's favourite. You mark out squares on the ground, and hop round kicking a stone from square to square. If the stone misses the right square, you're out.*

Most of the games here use objects that cost nothing, like sticks and stones.

Nomusa is cooking a big pot of a traditional Zulu dish: 'isijingi'. Tonight the weather's hot, so she prepares the meal outside. Everyone stops to watch.

Ten dinner plates piled high.

It's dinner time at last. And there's plenty for everyone!

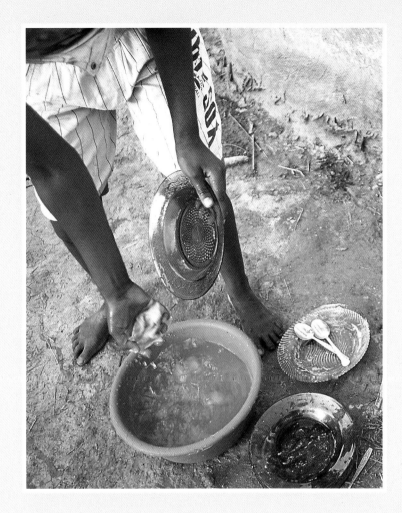

When the meal is over, the children clear away. They wash up under the cold tap beside the house, scrubbing the plates with their hands or a wet cloth until they are clean again.

The isijingi's gone now, every bit. There's just one part of the pumpkin left. Can you guess what it is?

1 **One** child, one seed to plant next time

1	one
2	two
3	three
4	four
5	five
6	six
7	seven
8	eight
9	nine
10	ten

More About South Africa

South Africa lies at the southern tip of the great continent of Africa. Nkandla, where Nothando lives, is in the north east of the country, about 50 miles from the Indian Ocean.

Tiny measurements on this map represent great distances in real life. South Africa is five times the size of Britain and more than 41 million people live there. The whole continent of Africa measures more than four thousand miles from north to south. The map shows 8 of Africa's 54 countries.

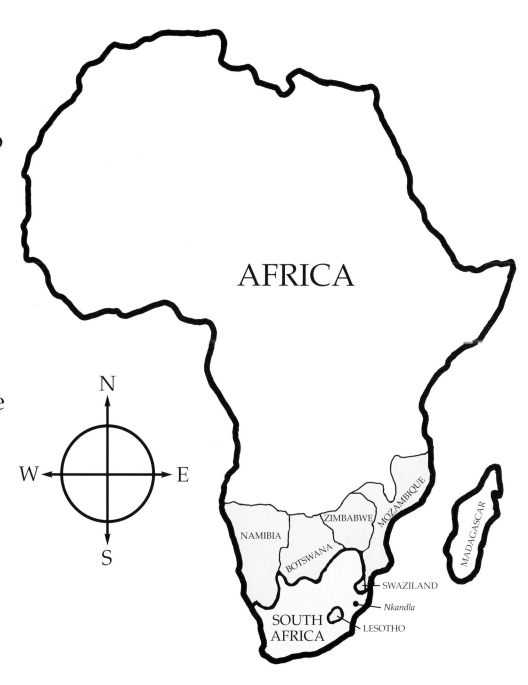

AFRICA

N

W   E

S

NAMIBIA
ZIMBABWE
MOZAMBIQUE
BOTSWANA
MADAGASCAR
SWAZILAND
Nkandla
SOUTH AFRICA
LESOTHO

Pumpkin Pie

Pumpkins can be cooked in lots of different ways. Pumpkin pie is a sweet dish that is eaten at Thanksgiving in the USA.

INGREDIENTS

250 g (8 oz) shortcrust pastry • 1 small pumpkin, weighing about 1.15 kg (2 ¾ lb)
2 eggs • 1 tin (400 g) sweetened condensed milk
1 teaspoon ground cinnamon • ½ teaspoon ground ginger
½ teaspoon ground nutmeg • ½ teaspoon salt

METHOD

1. Scoop the flesh out of the pumpkin, throwing away the skin and seeds.
2. Put the flesh in a pan, cover with water and simmer for 25 minutes, until tender.
3. Drain and leave to cool, then purée it in a blender or mash it, until it is free of lumps.
4. Preheat the oven to 200°C (400°F, Gas Mark 6)
5. Roll out the pastry on a lightly-floured work surface and use to line a 23 cm (9 inch) pie dish. Cover with greaseproof paper, fill with rice or baking beans and bake for 10 minutes.

6. Remove the paper and rice or beans, and return the dish to the oven for 5 minutes until the pastry is golden brown. Remove from the oven and reduce the heat to 190°C (375°F, Gas Mark 5).
7. In a large bowl, combine the pumpkin purée, eggs and sweetened condensed milk. Add the cinnamon, ginger, nutmeg and salt. Whisk together until thoroughly blended.
8. Pour into the pastry case and bake for 40 minutes until a knife inserted comes out clean.
9. Serve with whipped cream.

MORE TITLES BY FRANCES LINCOLN
IN ASSOCIATION WITH OXFAM

W is for World

Kathryn Cave

Stunning colour images from around the world invite children to
focus on the similarities as well as the differences between
other cultures and their own.

Suitable for Nursery Education and for
National Curriculum English – Reading, Key Stage 1
Scottish Guidelines English Language – Reading, Levels B and C;
Environmental Studies, Levels A, B and C

0-7112-1364-X   £5.99 (paperback)

Wake Up, World!

Beatrice Hollyer

Meet eight children from around the world as they eat, play,
go to school and talk about their dreams.

Suitable for Early Years Education and for National Curriculum English –
Reading, Key Stage 1; Geography, Key Stage 1
Scottish Guidelines English Language – Reading, Levels B and C;
Environmental Studies, Levels B and C

0-7112-1359-3   £12.99 (hardback)

Frances Lincoln titles are available from all good bookshops
Prices are correct at time of publication, but may be subject to change